NATIONAL GEOGRAPHIC

PIONEER EDITION

By Terrell Smith

CONTENTS

BY TERRELL SMITH

Dogs do all sorts of jobs. They help people at work and at home. These animals are doggone good workers!

Companion dog in Islip, New York

Working Like a Dog

Beagle Brigade in Miami, Florida

Dogs are called "man's best friends." That is because dogs are important to many people.

Some dogs are family pets. Others are trained to do special jobs. Dogs serve as "eyes" for the blind. Some working dogs are "ears" for the deaf.

Dogs do many other jobs too. They pull sleds. They sniff bags at airports. They even help the police find missing persons.

With the right training, dogs make great workers. They are smart and skilled. They also love people.

On the Job. *Azu (top) finds a missing fisherman in New York's Oswego River. Maggie, Jane, and Hobbs (middle) wait to rescue skiers in Colorado.*

Ski Patrol

SKI PATROL

FIRST AID

4

Need a Paw?

Some dogs help people in their daily lives. These dogs are called "service dogs." They help people who have physical **disabilities,** or problems with their bodies.

The dogs help the people do things they cannot do on their own. Some dogs open doors. They turn on lights. They pick up things.

The best known service dogs are guide dogs. They lead the **visually impaired,** or people who cannot see.

Helping Hearts

Service dogs can also help people live happier lives. That is the case for a girl named Megan.

Megan is seven. She has a disease called Angelman syndrome. Megan cannot speak or walk.

Megan once felt lonely. She had a hard time making friends. Then she got Gabri. The dog changed her life.

Now Gabri keeps Megan company. Making friends is easier too. People come right up to Megan and Gabri!

Noses That Know

Dogs do other kinds of work too. They have a better sense of smell than people do. So some dogs sniff bags at airports. They use their noses to find dangerous things. They might find bombs—or even bananas.

Yes, bananas. People are not allowed to bring certain foods into the United States. Fruits and other foods can carry insects and diseases. Dogs help keep these foods out of the country.

Dog Detectives

Some dogs use their noses to find people. Search-and-rescue (SAR) dogs search for missing people. They find lost hikers. Some SAR dogs save people after earthquakes. They find people under piles of rubble. How?

Dogs can smell tiny clues that people leave behind. These might be skin cells or hair. They could be bits of clothing. These clues lead an SAR dog to a missing person.

To the Rescue. *Nickie rides with workers to a collapsed building. Her super sense of smell will help the workers search for survivors.*

Good Breeding

Some **breeds,** or kinds, of dogs are good for certain jobs. Beagles are gentle and like finding hidden smells. So they are good airport workers. German shepherds are smart and loyal. They make good guide dogs.

A dog's breed might make it good at some things. Yet its personality is more important than its breed. For example, an SAR dog must be strong and smart. Most of all, it must love to play.

For SAR dogs, finding a person is a game of hide-and-seek. Yet to people, this "game" might be life or death.

You Call That Work?

SAR dogs have serious jobs. They save lives. Other dogs "work" at having fun.

Eagle loves bones, especially old ones. Eagle digs up bones of people who died hundreds of years ago.

Does this bother Eagle's owner? No! It actually helps him. He is an **archaeologist.** That is someone who studies the past. Eagle once helped him find an old cemetery.

Top Dog

Kersee may have the best career of all. This dog is a Vice President at Iams. That is a pet-food company. Kersee goes to important events. She also welcomes people who visit Iams.

Movie Stars.
These dogs look relaxed. But they are really acting in a movie.

Pooch Paychecks

Dogs do great work. What do they get in return? They do not get cash. Their pay is love, food, shelter, and good care. Dogs depend on people. People also depend on their dogs.

Wordwise

archaeologist: scientist who learns about ancient people by studying what they left behind

breed: kind of dog

disability: inability to do something, such as walk or see

visually impaired: blind or unable to see well

AT YOUR

SERVICE

Service dogs help people in many ways. How do these dogs get ready for their full-time jobs? They get a lot of training.

The training serves them well. The dogs learn many skills. They also get confidence. That is important. After all, people's lives are in their paws.

What do the dogs learn in training? It depends on the job. Let's find out how guide dogs are trained. These dogs help the visually impaired.

JOHN T. MILLER

Step 1

Guide dogs start their training early. They are just eight weeks old. What can a puppy learn? It learns to love people. It learns to sit and stay. It learns to behave like a good dog!

Step 2

Later, the dog's training gets harder. A trainer works with the dog every day. The dog learns to listen and obey. The trainer says, "Halt." The dog stops.

The dog learns how to stay safe. It learns how to cross a street. It looks both ways for cars.

Step 3

Next, the dog learns to lead. It guides its trainer around town. The dog also learns when not to listen. The dog should not cross a street in front of a car. No matter what the trainer says!

Step 4

Soon the dog finishes training. Then it must pass some tests. The trainer puts on a blindfold. The dog leads the trainer up stairs. It crosses busy streets. The tests make sure a dog is ready for its job. Soon the guide dog will "see" for someone who is visually impaired.

PONY GUIDES

Tiny ponies are another kind of service animal. They can lead people who are visually impaired.

STEVEN SENNE, AP/WIDE WORLD PHOTOS

Pint-size Ponies. *This tiny horse guides a man who is visually impaired.*

11

Service Dogs

Can you sniff out the answers to these questions from the book?

1 How can dogs help people with disabilities?

2 Why do dogs work at airports?

3 What is a search-and-rescue dog?

4 How does one dog help an archaeologist discover the past?

5 Why is a service dog's training so important?